Additional Publications
by Victor Kwegyir

Quotable Quotes For Business:
Lessons For Success
(Pathway to Business Success Series)
by Victor Kwegyir

Beyond The Passion:
What It Takes To Achieve Success In Business
(Pathway to Business Success Series)
by Victor Kwegyir

Pitch Your Business Like A Pro:
Mastering The Art Of Winning Investor Support For Business
Success
(Pathway to Business Success Series)
by Victor Kwegyir

The Business You Can Start:
Spotting The Greatest Opportunities In The
Economic Downturn
(Pathway to Business Success Series)
by Victor Kwegyir

You've Been Fired! Now What?
Seize The Opportunity, Creatively
Turn It Into A Successful Reality
by Tonia Askins and Victor Kwegyir

THE BUSINESS YOU CAN START

WORKBOOK

CREATING THE GREATEST OPPORTUNITIES

FOR A SUCCESSFUL BUSINESS

Practical exercises for getting
YOU started in business

VICTOR KWEGYIR — MSC

INTERNATIONAL BUSINESS CONSULTANT, COACH, MENTOR & SPEAKER

THE BUSINESS YOU CAN START WORKBOOK
Copyright © 2017 by Victor Kwegyir

Published by Vike Springs Publishing Ltd.
www.vikesprings.com

The Business You Can Start – Workbook Edition
ISBN - 978-1-9998509-0-6 - EBook
ISBN - 978-1-9998509-1-3 - Paperback

PATHWAY TO BUSINESS SUCCESS SERIES
Printed in the United Kingdom
and the United States of America

To request Victor for speaking engagements,
interviews, mentoring, proposal writing, ghost writing and publishing,
coaching or consultation
services, please send an email to:
admin@vikesprings.com

*Victor's books are available at special discounts when purchased in bulk for promotions or
as donations for educational and training purposes.*

Limit of Liability/Disclaimer of Warranty

Dedication

I dedicate this book to all entrepreneurs and business owners committed to delivering quality products, excellent services and creating wealth for their generation.

Acknowledgments

I am grateful to everyone who has been there for this journey and to everyone who has inspired me with their encouragement and helped me to put this fifth publication together, another exciting resource for entrepreneurs, business owners and aspiring entrepreneurs.

I am always grateful to God for continued mercies, strength, wisdom and ability to do what I do; to my pastor, Pastor Matthew Ashimolowo, President and Senior Pastor of Kingsway International Christian Centre (KICC), for continued inspiration to strive for excellence and explore possibilities to make an impact in our generation; to all my great friends and family who have been a great network of support to me in my journey; Michael Ajose, Mrs. Kemba Agard, Mr Wyn Knucles, to Pastor Ade D'Almeida – KICC, and to my entire family for their prayers, encouragement and support. You have all contributed in many ways to make this a reality. I appreciate you.

THANK YOU all once again!!!

Introduction

To have picked this book tells me you may have been inspired by the desire to consider a career change or start off your own business; be it for extra income, a threat of job loss or already lost your job.

Conversely you may not have thought of any of the reasons stated above. Regardless of your situation, this book is one you must own!

This is a complementary workbook to be used with the original book "The Business You Can Start - Spotting The Greatest Opportunities In The Economic Downturn". It challenges and inspires you to take a second look at the economy anywhere in the world and see rare business opportunities staring you right in the face that you can take full advantage of.

This book is a practical guide to starting and growing a business. It will help you uncover the secrets that have transformed the lives of many successful business owners as well as inspire and challenge you to identify new business opportunities.

It is structured and designed simply for the users' greatest flexibility.

The marketplace richly rewards entrepreneurs for the problems they solve. Think of that and let this book show you how to take your share of what the market has on offer.

The reward is always far more than the sacrifice, no matter how small the start may seem. If for nothing at all, just try something but don't give up! You will deny yourself the numerous possibilities if you fail to try when the opportunity is presented to you. Life can only offer so much, you are the only one who can determine how much of that will be yours.

Contents

Chapter I

Should I or Can I Start a Business?

"Two sure ways to fail - think and never do or do and never think."

– Zig Ziglar
Author and Motivational Speaker

If you are among those who already have settled in their hearts, not only in their minds, to start a business, I commend you for making such a decision. It's a great step forward because the process of being able to make firm decisions is essential in any kind of business undertaking. As General George S. Patton, who served in both World Wars said,

"Be willing to make decisions. That's the most important quality in a good leader."

This workbook, plus its companion text "THE BUSINESS YOU CAN START – Spotting The Greatest Opportunities In The Economic Downturn", is your best bet in making the next strategic move in this direction.

For others, the challenge is the thought of having to take initiative and answer the questions:

- when is the right time?
- how do I start?
- what is the right approach?

To these people, I say keep reading and I will help you to find answers to these questions.

There is another group of people who have started a business which is now perceived to have failed. Some in this group will have a lingering desire to try again, while others might have resigned themselves to their fate. To those people, I will agree with Robert H. Schuller, who once said,

"Failure doesn't mean you are a failure it just means you haven't succeeded yet."

The Benefits of Starting A Business

"Traditional thinking is all about 'what is.' Future thinking will also need to be about 'what can be'."

So let me ask you, why do YOU want to start a business?

There is nothing more important than being clear on your reasons for taking action because when things get difficult or do not adhere to your plan, and believe me, this will happen, you will need to remind yourself why you got started in the business in the first place.

Many of the common reasons why people want to start their own business are listed below. Some of these will apply to you, others may not. Take your time and think about each one. In the spaces below, write why each reason is or is not important to you.

You are **your own** boss. You get to be in control, directing your business the way you want it in line with your dreams.

You get to manage your time better to suit your personal life.

You have flexibility. Flexibility allows you to change course or adapt quickly to new opportunities without anyone else's approval. There is therefore no need to feed ideas up any chain of command.

You have no limit on the amount of income you earn. In fact, you get to determine the pace of growth of your income in line with your capacity to produce.

You set your own goals, having no limit to how successful you'll want to be.

You have job security. You are relieved of the thought of ever being "fired." The challenge is to ensure that your business runs profitably and smoothly.

You have the ability to create wealth and influence society.

You have a reduction in personal liability, especially in the case of setting up as a Limited Liability Company.

Businesses, in many instances, are deemed to be separate entities from their owners and directors and have a perpetual existence. They can therefore be passed on to your children whereas you cannot do so with your job.

By having your own business, you have a sense of ownership, destiny, and can have a better life as the business pays for these benefits. For instance, as a business grows the business can buy cars, properties, etc, for the use of its directors, and expenses are charged to the business accounts.

Stemming from the above are tax liabilities, which are largely reduced because several expenses you would have paid off from your salary can be dealt with as company expenses.

A company can live beyond you and be able to generate income even in your old age.

Owning a business gives you an opportunity of a lifetime to be an employer, thus influencing positively the lives of others and society at large.

You feel personal achievement. The joy derived from creating and running a successful business can be exhilarating. As your business grows, the satisfaction of knowing that you did it from the ground up is far more fulfilling than building someone else's business.

Through your company, you can give to various causes of your choice, charities, educational institutions, etc. Especially for those who are passionate about various charitable causes, there is no joy comparable to setting up your own business and generating the income and profits to fund your vision without being reliant on others.

You are a problem solver. As a business owner, your products or services provide solutions for your clients and society at large. As a solution provider, you earn respect in your community and nation.

Now write down the most important reasons why you want to start your own business.

Starting A Business In An Economic Downturn

History has taught us that innovative ideas are born as a solution to challenging times. Most of the billiondollar businesses out there today were established during the Great Depression and the recessionary years of the 1950s, '70s, '80s, and '90s.

"Challenging economic times can serve as a motivational boost to individuals who have been laid-off to become their own employers and future job creators," Carl Schramm, president and CEO at Kauffman

But economic downturn is not necessarily a barrier to starting a new business. Instead they bring with it some opportune conditions, which when exploited, can be a great platform for the start and growth of a business.

Open your eyes, decide to look at things differently, determine to start something and make a smart and informed move towards one kind of business or the other. With the right practical steps, you will get hold of your dreams and turn them into reality.

What opportunities have you identified in the current economic situation that will impact on YOUR business?

1.

2.

3.

4.

5.

"Don't wait until everything is just right. It will never be perfect. There will always be challenges, obstacles and less than perfect conditions. So what? Get started now. With each step you take, you will grow stronger and stronger, more and more self-confident and more and more successful,"

Mark Victor Hansen.

Chapter 2

Spotting Ideas and Identifying Opportunities

"Capital isn't that important in business. Experience isn't that important. You can get both of these things. What is important are ideas."

– Harvey S. Firestone
Founder of Firestone Tire and Rubber Company

You have made that all-important decision from the previous chapter to start a business. Some of you might already have a kind of business in mind at this stage, while others have yet to decide on a particular line of business. At whatever stage you are, this chapter will help you fine-tune and define clearly the way forward with what kind of business will be best for you.

So, to get started, write down a list of all the ideas you have for a business. I want you to do this to clear your mind and free yourself for more creative thinking. Don't worry if you have no ideas at the moment, this chapter will help you to spot opportunities and find new ideas.

1. ....

2. ....

3. ....

4. ....

5. ....

Whether you already have ideas for a business or not, let's change focus and think about developing new ideas based on your skills, strengths, interests and hobbies.

Use existing skills from past employment.

This is where we challenge you to use your skills and experience that you acquired while working in your current or previous employment to meet the needs of a niche market. You may be able to provide a product or service being sourced by your current place of employment better than a current supplier.

What skills do YOU have?

Skill #1 ....

How could you use this skill to create a business?

....
....
....
....
....

Skill #2 ....

How could you use this skill to create a business?

....
....
....
....
....

Skill #3 ....

How could you use this skill to create a business?

....
....
....
....
....

Use your personality for a business idea.

Are you a good communicator? Could you be a good salesperson?

Are you an outstanding networker? Could you be a person who makes everyone feel at home anytime anywhere?

Or are you a collector of a kind and could you sell products online to a niche market?

These examples should give you a fair idea of what to do and where to start.
So take a moment to think about your top FIVE strengths and what ideas do you have to capitalise on them.

Strength #1 ....

How could you use this strength in your business?

How could you use this strength in your business?

Strength #2 ....

How could you use this strength in your business?

Strength #3 ....

How could you use this strength in your business?

```
..............................................................................................
..............................................................................................
..............................................................................................
..............................................................................................
..............................................................................................
```

Turn your hobby into a viable business.

Can you find creative ways of making money out of your hobby? Basing your business idea around something you enjoy doing is one of the surest ways of succeeding.

Passion and enthusiasm sells better than just introducing a product.
What hobbies or interests do you have?

Hobby/Interest #1 ....

How could you turn this hobby or interest into a business?

```
..............................................................................................
..............................................................................................
..............................................................................................
..............................................................................................
..............................................................................................
..............................................................................................
..............................................................................................
```

Hobby/Interest #2 ....

How could you turn this hobby or interest into a business?

....

....

....

....

Hobby/Interest #3 ....

How could you turn this hobby or interest into a business?

....

....

....

....

Still struggling to find ideas? What follows is a list of things that could trigger your creativity and open your mind to new business opportunities. I suggest that you grab a pen and read through the list. There is space at the end of each item for you to write down ideas that hit you as you read.

Have a closer look at current social trends. Social trends could be a source of opportunities to explore. For example, more people are getting married later than before so there are a lot more single parents and nearly one-third of men and one-fifth of women aged twenty to thirty-four live with their parents.

There are many other trends to exploit included in "THE BUSINESS YOU CAN START – Spotting The Greatest Opportunities In The Economic Downturn".

Your ideas

Provide services that make others feel good. As an example, "a junk clearance service," is a service that helps people simplify and declutter their lives and at the same time helps them to give back to their communities. You can check on such websites as www. anyjunk.co.uk and this book "Global Ideas Bank" available on Amazon for more details.

Your ideas

Become a tour guide or set up a leisure business in your area. For instance, open a tea shop for an area with high population of pensioners or in one that attracts high influx of tourists. Open an outdoor centre in a rural area. Talking to your local council, tourist board, Regional Development Agencies (RDAs), or municipal assembly may give you an idea of priority areas they might already have identified due to research, policy focus, etc.

Your ideas

....

....

....

....

....

....

Explore the possibility of using latest technology to create a business. The lifestyle of the 21st century thrives much on technology, and there seems to be no end to new ones popping up each day. Facebook, Twitter, Instagram, Pinterest, to name a few, are examples of these. www.cartoonstock.com may also offer you some ideas.

Your ideas

....

....

....

....

....

....

Look into your backyard. Identify problems and difficulties that you have experienced in getting things for your home, work, or in your leisure activities.

- ◇ Is there any service you need that is not available locally?
- ◇ Is there any part of a product that is almost impossible
- ◇ to obtain locally?
- ◇ Are there any issues that attract most complaints from
- ◇ your neighbours, friends, and even visitors to your locality?

- ◇ Are there any problems that cause you so much inconvenience and are much more costly to solve?

Your ideas

Ask questions. Listen to people's problems, hopes, dreams, and aspirations. There are often good business opportunities in solving challenges people face in their businesses or jobs.

Your ideas

Sell other people's goods. It's a known fact that many new firms start off by selling goods that somebody else produced and there are a lot of opportunities to distribute foreign goods in any given country. Look at www.buyusa.gov/uk/en for more information. Chambers of commerce and other trade bodies around the world also publish regular listings of businesses seeking partners willing to manufacture under licence or to act as sole distributors.

Your ideas

....

....

....

....

....

....

....

....

Research local authorities, large firms, and other public bodies in your area. Get to know what they make and components of their raw materials that they buy from outside the area and see if you can supply such components. You can check out www.direct.gov. uk and www.usa.gov to locate the contact details of your local council or government.

See www.supply2.gov.uk for an overview of the purchasing procedure of public authorities. And, more recently, a lot more websites are being created by local and municipal assemblies publishing budget plans and general operational policies, which are all a great source for business ideas.

Your ideas

Look out for potential labour shortages in your area or even overseas. Pursuit of academic qualifications other than the more traditional vocational training left many skilled shortages for traditional trades. Most of these office workers and even professionals have retrained as plumbers, mechanics, etc, and started their own businesses because of the shortages and the financial rewards that come with it. You could investigate your area for any such possible skill shortages.

Your ideas

Identify opportunities by watching the news. Newspapers, magazines, online discussion forums, blogs, and e-zines are all fruitful sources of new and emerging trends and problems that need a solution. Small advertisement sections of local papers are a good way to get an idea of local patterns of supply and demand. Read the business opportunities sections in the national and local newspapers. Eli Broad, an American philanthropist and founder of Kaufman & Broad (now KB Home) and financial giant SunAmerica (now a subsidiary of AIG) once said,

"There is no substitute for knowledge. To this day, I read three newspapers a day. It is impossible to read a paper without being exposed to ideas. And ideas... more than money... are the real currency for success."

Your ideas

> ....
> ....
> ....

Copy business ideas that have taken off elsewhere. A lot of business ideas originate from abroad and get established locally. You can pick up on a trend and be the first to offer that product or service in your local area. For example, the founder of Kwik-Fit, Tom Farmer, got the idea from the 'muffler shops' he saw on a visit to the US. The decline in the popularity of DIY led to entrepreneurs in London offering a niche service assembling flat-pack furniture for customers. Websites like www.handylocals.com may help you.

Your ideas

> ....
> ....
> ....

Keep up with changes in the laws of the land. New policies and legislation are often a rich source of new business ideas. They always generate opportunities in terms of administration and implementation. New safety or health regulation requirements may prompt the supply of parts to adapt an existing process to meet the standards, or a demand for people to provide a newly introduced service. For example, the introduction of the new Home Information Packs for buyers and sellers of domestic properties from June 2007 in the UK got people training for the Home Inspector qualification, which qualified them to carry out inspections for the Energy Performance Certificate and the voluntary Home Condition Report. Keep track of legislation from parliaments and legislative bodies locally, nationally, and around the world for information on new legislation. For examples, visit www.opsi.gov.uk and www. us.gov.

Your ideas

....

....

....

....

Buy an existing business. Local papers and relevant trade magazines usually advertise businesses for sale. The following sources regularly advertise updated business opportunities: www.loot. com, www.uk.businessesforsale.com, www.daltonsbusiness. com.

Your ideas

```
..................................................................................................................
..................................................................................................................
..................................................................................................................
..................................................................................................................
```

Go into franchising. You get the independence and satisfaction of running your own venture but benefit from marketing support and an established customer base. The following web links provide more information and opportunity listings for franchising: www.franinfo.co.uk, www.franchiseexpo.co.uk, www.thebfa.org, www.whichfranchise.com.

Your ideas

```
..................................................................................................................
..................................................................................................................
..................................................................................................................
..................................................................................................................
```

Identify products and services to export. Look out for products or services that are working in your current city or country of residence and export to other countries that lack such products or services.

Your ideas

```
..................................................................................................................
..................................................................................................................
..................................................................................................................
..................................................................................................................
```

Use all the research tools you can find. Surveys, consumer market research, and government statistics are all available online and are easily accessible. You could also get to know of gaps in the market and useful network opportunities. Most local libraries have countless information on this.

Your ideas

Visit exhibitions and trade shows. Major exhibitions are usually packed full of start-up ideas, mostly aimed at people who are seeking to become self-employed. Check www.exhibitions. co.uk, www.tradeshow.globalsources.co, www.eventseye.com and www.expocentral.com for shows across the globe.

Your ideas

Work as a freelancer. Many more people are choosing to work flexibly from home or outside the traditional employment system. As a freelancer, you can often choose to work from home or in various places to cover absent staff or to help with the peaks and troughs in established businesses. Some professional and experienced managers have set up businesses as an interim, working on short-term assignments or projects at other firms. Check out information and job listings for freelancers at www.freelancers.net, www.freelanceuk.com, www.upworks.com and www.toptal.com.

Your ideas

> ....
> ....
> ....
> ....

Invent something. Every year, around 20,000 people in the UK apply for patents, with 20 percent of these applications made by individuals rather than businesses or institutions. You could get more information from the UK, USA, EU and other Intellectual Property Offices around the world by visiting www.ipo.gov.uk, www.uspto.gov, www.ec.europa.eu/internal_market/copyright, www.wipo.int, and www.patentlawlinks.com. There are companies that could also help you develop your inventions. My advice is to thoroughly research the best and get good protection and agreements before you make your idea known to them.

Your ideas

> ....
> ....
> ....
> ....

Take advantage to cash in on the 'time poor.' You could start a business that meets the needs of professional and busy people who have little time available to themselves. Many kinds of business ideas fall under this category, from simple ones such as personal shopping and dog walking to many of the Internet-based businesses such as selling items on ebay and other auction sites for others.

Your ideas

Simply improve on an existing product or service. You could simply look out for products or services you have a passion toward to improve on their quality, value, effectiveness, efficiency, reliability, and much more.

Your ideas

Launch an accidental business. First and foremost, you create something that you'll love working on even if it never takes off and eventually becomes loved by other people. What, rather perversely, is also the best way to make sure it's something cool enough and passion-filled enough to grow that loyal audience? Build a community around it. Then, finally, try to figure out how to make some cash from it.

Your ideas

....
....
....
....
....
....

Look ahead. What do you believe consumers will want or be looking out for in three to six months from now, a year from now, that they can't find today on the market? Future trends are a big thing these days. The Henry Ford's (Ford Motors), Sir Tim Berners-Lee (World Wide Web), Bill Gates (Microsoft PC), Steve Jobs (Apple), Mark Zuckerberg (Facebook), Larry Page and Sergey Brin (Google), and many others have and still look to project the needs of consumers ahead of time.

Your ideas

....
....
....
....
....

Fund other people's ideas. You may be someone who has resources but no time to get involved in the day-to-day running of business. You could make available your cash to others with great ideas but with no resources.

Your ideas

....

....

....

....

....

Invest in stocks. There are various opportunities in trading in stocks both for short-term and long-term gains. From spread betting and derivatives to simple buying and selling of shares, I have a three-part article on my blog (http://vikeinvest-life. blogspot.com/) on ground rules for investing that will help you immensely.

Your ideas

....

....

....

....

....

Write for cash. How about writing for cash? You can contribute to various established blogging sites and get paid. Or you could create a blog of your own, write interesting stuff, simply build a great following, and with Google Adsense, you could be on your way into making some good money. Just start by searching online for some of these sites: www.ezinearticles.com, www. hubpages.com, and www.blogger.com.

Your ideas

....

....

....

....

....

....

If you are still struggling for ideas, try these interesting websites
www.entrepreneur.com
www.businessopportunitiesandideas.com
www.trendwatching.com

Before we move on to the next chapter, pick your top idea for YOUR future business. Don't make any judgement about how good or bad the idea is at this point, just write it down.

My business idea is

....

....

....

....

....

....

....

Chapter 3

Steps in Developing an Idea

*"If you have ideas, you have the main asset
you need, and there isn't any limit to what
you can do with your business and your life.
Ideas are any man's greatest assets."*

– Harvey S. Firestone
Founder of Firestone Tire and Rubber Company

A good new idea is often the basis for starting up a business. From the previous chapter, we have established that you could spot a gap in the market and start a business that provides a product or service to fill it or come up with ways to improve an existing product.

The next step is to develop the idea into a viable product or service.

With the idea you came up with in Chapter 2, ask yourself these questions.

Does my business idea meet a specific need? If yes, can you state the need?

```
..................................................................................
..................................................................................
..................................................................................
..................................................................................
```

Is it an answer to a specific question? If yes, can you state the question ?

```
..................................................................................
..................................................................................
..................................................................................
..................................................................................
```

Is it a solution to a specific problem? If yes, can you state the specific problem?

```
..................................................................................
..................................................................................
..................................................................................
..................................................................................
```

Can I offer something different from what may already be in existence? If yes, what would be your difference?

Is what I want to offer going out of fashion, trend, or being taken over by new technology? If yes, how can it affect what you want to offer?

Is it a regulated business, and can I meet the requirements in a cost-effective way? If it is, what are the requirements you must meet and at what cost?

Can I produce the item or provide the service at a reasonable cost? If yes, how much would it cost per unit?

Can I put a price on my products or services? If yes, at what price?

Are people willing to pay for it?

Can I make a profit at the acceptable price or price people are willing to pay for my products or services? If yes, at what profit margin?

Let us now consider a few steps that can help you fine-tune an idea into a fully-fledged viable business idea.

Try to learn something new every day. Having conceived an idea or two, it may be necessary to talk to other businesspeople, friends, neighbours, if possible, anyone who looks interesting and will talk to you about what you are considering and possibly give feedback on what they think. However, exercise a lot of discretion in knowing who to talk to. In the words of **Thomas Berger**,

"The art and science of asking questions is the source of all knowledge."

Browse the web, and read magazines, books, and biographies of businesspeople, expanding your knowledge each day on the ideas.

What did you learn today?

....

....

....

....

....

....

....

Keep a written record of your ideas. Whenever you are inspired by an idea, write it down. There is no limit to the number of ideas you can write down. You are more likely to remember them and can always refer to them should you forget. Writing down any idea that comes to mind can help you differentiate between ideas. It's very important to be as specific as possible at this stage. For instance, an idea such as "A Clothing or Book Store" is different from "Online Clothing or Book Store."

Draw a mind map. Often, to have a pictorial view of how your idea is coming together, drawing a mind map is a very good way to go. A mind map is simply a diagram used to represent words and, ideas, linked to and arranged around a central key word or idea. It helps to generate, visualise, structure, and classify ideas. It also acts as an aid in study, organisation, problem solving, decision making, and writing.

Make a mind map of your idea here.

Research other conditions out there. Evaluate potential competition, keeping notes on what you find. A thorough assessment and market research at this stage will help you to establish whether there is a market for your product or service. Answer the questions below to determine with your business idea in mind.

Is this product or service I have in mind going to satisfy a market need?

What competition is out there? Is it direct or indirect, local, national, or international?

....
....
....
....

How distinct is my product from what is being offered by the competition?

....
....
....
....

Can the product stand the test of changing trends or take advantage of it before it dies out?

....
....
....
....

Does the law of the land allow for such a business to be established?

....
....
....
....
....
....

At what prices are consumers prepared to buy my product, and can I make any profit at any stage?

> ....
> ....
> ....
> ....

Synthesise ideas. Putting two or more unrelated ideas together and brainstorm it. For instance, setting up a bookstore to providing courier service or selling clothes online to offering a professional secretarial or accountancy service or manufacturing a new brand of fruit juice to importing rice, etc. That helps to make a firm decision on the way forward.

Do you have any ideas that could be merged to create a new business?

> ....
> ....
> ....
> ....

Sleep on the idea. Go away for a while, thinking of something else. Often your subconscious mind will continue to work on the problem and will come up with new ideas or refinements to the original idea.

Talk about your ideas. Talk especially with those close to you and who have your interest at heart. Brainstorm your idea with friends, colleagues, or staff. They can give different perspectives on the idea and may know if there is anyone else doing the same thing out there. In the words of Robert Quillen, *"Discussion is an exchange of knowledge."* Write down how you would explain your idea to another person. This helps you spot flaws or areas for improvement.

Consider impact of new technologies. Given the pace of technological advancement, you may need to think about whether your idea can take advantage of an opportunity created by any new technology available or even yet to be developed. An example is online trading instead of the more traditional way of trading at a fixed location.

How does new technology impact on your business idea?

Consider impact of social trends. It is also very important to consider whether social trends may affect the design or demand for your product or service. Examples are concerns about global warming and carbon footprints, or increasing demand for organic food.

What social trends impact on your business idea?

Write your business plan. Inasmuch as I will not insist on you writing a business plan before you start, the comprehensive guide I have provided in this book can help you realistically assess the viability and potential success of your idea and chosen business model and processes. *See appendix for a full Business Plan Template.*

Protect your idea. You should confine and protect your idea. Keep your idea as private as possible except, of course, with the trusted and respected individuals who are part of the process of development. It will be smart to stop talking about your idea once you have finalised on the specific one to pursue, until such time as its ready for the market and any licensing necessary to protect the idea has been secured to protect your ownership. It takes wisdom to know when to speak and when to shut up.

In Summary

Whatever idea you decide on, it is critical that you
- clearly understand how you think your intended business will work
- identify who your customers are going to be
- know what problem you are going to solve
- know how your product or service is going to meet the needs
- know how will your customers find your product to buy
- know who will sell it
- know who will deliver it

You must also have clearly stated objectives of how you intend to achieve them and succeed with it.

This chapter has helped you to fine-tune your business idea. In the next chapter, we will highlight a few factors that, when taken into consideration, can help put you on "top of the game" with your idea as you enter the market.

Chapter 4

Creating a Distinction for Your Product or Service

"You're just anybody without your identity."

– Grenville Main
MD of DNA Design

Having gone through the basic steps in fine-tuning your idea, let us look at how you are going to distinguish yourself from the existing market.

What is your Unique Selling Point (USP)?

In the words of Tom Chappell, an American businessman and manufacturer,

> *"Success means never letting the competition define you. Instead you have to define yourself based on a point of view you care deeply about."*

Establishing your USP is very important. It should focus on how your product or service will benefit the customer and what makes you totally stand out from the competition. This can be summed up in just a few words that become something like a catchphrase of your advertising jingle. It may also be expressed as a summary of what you do and how you do it better or differently than others. Do everything possible not to be tempted to choose a phrase that becomes counterproductive because you could not fulfil the promise. Your USP also helps protect your idea in the marketplace.

Establish your uniqueness by answering these questions.

What are the core needs of your customers and market?

Are there any untapped areas in your market and if so, how can you exploit them?

How can you take advantage of technology and the Internet to enhance your business?

How can you take advantage of established systems and build on them without needing to start from scratch?

What is going to be your specialty or niche area?

Who are your customers? Look at the demographics: age, gender, interests, location, national or international markets, etc.

What do these customers want? Is it a kind of flexible service, low prices, availability of your product or service locally, trusted source, or something else that will attract customers to your business?

How are you going to do it? Will there be something special, unusual, or significant about the way you will do business? Fast turnaround, free delivery, personal service, etc?

Developing Your Brand

"A brand is not saying what it is, it's what the customer THINKS it is."
Karen Katz, CEO of Neiman Marcus

Closely associated with USP is branding. Unfortunately, most people start their businesses without thinking about either.

Take a minute to think about the brands you are most familiar with. Write down as many as you can.

What do these brands have in common?

1.

2.

3.

4.

5.

Now let's examine what specific things that you will need to focus on to ensure that you build a strong brand for YOUR business?

A memorable and easy-to-remember brand name

What is your business name? Is it easy to pronounce and remember? Does it suggest the product's benefits and uses? Is it attractive and does it stand out against the competition?

A professionally designed distinctive logo

Do you have a logo for your business? If not, what steps do you need to take to create one for your business? Consider colour, size and quality of the image.

A catchy phrase or slogan

Do you have a slogan for your business? If not, what steps do you need to take to create one for your business?

Professionally designed stationery

There are a lot of free business card offers on the Internet. However, the quality of the materials and processing are mostly below standard. A little search-and-spend will get you a professionally designed quality logo, business card, and letterhead, often offered as a complete package, which communicate value and seriousness to potential businesses and clients.

What steps do you need to take to create professional stationery for your business? Remember to include business cards, letterheads, website and flyers or brochures.

Strategic advertising

What are the steps that you need to take to develop a strategic advertising plan for your business? Have you considered social media, local and national newspapers, radio, television, Google Adwords? Don't forget the power of word of mouth.

As a new business, obviously there might not be enough money to embark on all these right from the start. However, the purpose at this stage is to have all these factors in mind so that if you can only afford to do one, you do not just do anything just for the sake of it.

"A brand is a living entity—and it is enriched or undermined cumulatively over time, the product of a thousand small gestures"
(Michael Eisner, Disney CEO).

Protecting Your Brand

To protect your brand, it must be properly trademarked, ensuring that other people cannot use your brand for their gain. You can trademark words, names, logos, or designs or a combination of these. A trademark will give a business an exclusive right to use the trademark and may lawfully prosecute any parties that use the same trademark in the future.

For a business name to be trademarked in most jurisdictions or countries it may have to be established through actual use in the marketplace, or through registration of the mark with the trademarks office or trademarks registry in that country or jurisdiction. However, in some jurisdictions trademark rights may be established through either or both means. There is more information about registering a company name in different jurisdictions in "THE BUSINESS YOU CAN START – Spotting The Greatest Opportunities In The Economic Downturn"

What are the steps that you need to protect your brand?

1.

2.

3.

4.

5.

Chapter 5

What Business Model Should I Adopt?

"Whenever you see a successful business, someone once made a courageous decision."

– Peter Drucker
Writer and Management Consultant

A business model is simply the plan implemented by a company to generate revenue and make a profit from operations. It includes the components and functions of the business, as well as the revenues it generates and the expenses it incurs. There are different aspects and kinds of models that a business can adopt.

Many of the advantages and disadvantages of the models are discussed in "THE BUSINESS YOU CAN START – Spotting The Greatest Opportunities In The Economic Downturn". Refer to this before answering the questions.

Home-Based Business

This is one of the most common models adopted by new small businesses. The flexibility, freedom, and minimal start-up cost associated with this model as well as advances in technology in respect of improved communication tools and the Internet have made having an office at home even more practical.

What are the advantages of a home-based business for you?

What are the disadvantages of a home-based business for you?

What steps do you need to take to establish a home-based business?

Bricks & Mortar

That is, starting from a designated office, store, shop, premises, etc.

What are the advantages of a bricks & mortar business for you?

What are the disadvantages of a bricks & mortar business for you?

What steps do you need to take to establish a bricks & mortar business?

E-Commerce

Web-based businesses are the norm now and not the exception any more. The volume of business transacted via this model has grown extraordinarily with wide-spread Internet usage.

What are the advantages of an e-commerce business for you?

What are the disadvantages of an e-commerce business for you?

What steps do you need to take to establish an e-commerce business?

Licensing A Product

Licensing is a way of commercialising your invention. It involves signing a product licensing deal with another company, granting them the permission to make use of the intellectual property rights of your invention. It's basically the process of leasing your right to an idea or product to another business entity in return for royalty. This intellectual property right may be for a patent, trade secret, copyright, technical know-how, or a trademark.

A good licensing agreement must touch on the exclusivity, market, territory, terms of royalty payments, rights to modify and combine with other products, transfer and sublicense rights, limitations on liability audits rights and reporting, prohibited uses, guaranteed annual minimum royalty, advance payment, indemnity, and termination.

What are the advantages of licensing a product for you?

What are the disadvantages of licensing a product for you?

What steps do you need to take to build licensing into your business model?

Multi-Level Marketing

Multi-level marketing is a business model where the businessperson or distributor buys products of an existing established business, sells them, and gets compensated or receives commission not only for sales personally made but also for the sales of others they recruit to join their distribution network. This creates levels of distributors in a hierarchy for multiple levels of compensation.

The distributor markets these products directly to consumers by means of relationships, referrals, and word of mouth. A distributor has basically two responsibilities: first, to sell the company's products, and second, to recruit more distributors to join the hierarchy to sell the company's products.

What are the advantages of multi-level marketing for you?

What are the disadvantages of multi-level marketing for you?

_____

What steps do you need to build multi-level market into your business model?

_____

Drop Shipping

Another model that has recently gained popularity is drop shipping. With this model, the retailer does not keep goods in stock but takes orders and forwards customer orders and shipment details to either the wholesaler or manufacturer, who then ships the goods directly to the customer. Stocking the products is the prime responsibility of the wholesaler or manufacturer and not the retailer. The retailer makes his or her money, as in any business, between the retail and wholesale price.

_____

What are the disadvantages of drop shipping for you?

What steps do you need to take to build drop shipping into your business model?

In the next chapter we will consider and analyse the next most important decision to make in starting your own business.

Chapter 6

Which Legal Structure Will Best Suit Me?

"In modern business it is not the crook who is to be feared most, it is the honest man who doesn't know what he is doing."

– William Wordsworth

It is important to make an informed decision on the right legal structure of the business you want to set up. There are a number of legal structures, all of which differ in several aspects.

For simplification and consistency, I am adopting the United Kingdom legal structure as the basis for this chapter. However, there are a number of similarities in the underlying principles around the world.

Your choice of legal structure will affect many things including your tax liability, the level of risk and control you will have and the way management decisions are made in respect of the business.

We will look at the common features of each of the common business structures and the advantages and disadvantages of adopting each. Other important considerations, including the features and benefits of each legal structure you should consider, are discussed in "THE BUSINESS YOU CAN START – Spotting The Greatest Opportunities In The Economic Downturn".

Sole Trader

This is the most common structure adopted by new business owners. It is the simplest way to run a business, as you are the only person legally responsible for the running of the business.

What are the steps you would need to take to set up a sole trader business model?

I.

2.

3.

4.

5.

Partnership

This is the next most popular legal structure adopted. It is a relatively simple and flexible way for two or more people to own and run a business. However, each partner is regarded as self-employed, and there is no formal registration process with this structure. Partners usually share in the decision-making process.

Are you considering the Partnership structure? If so, why?

What steps would you need to take to set up a partnership business model?

1.
....

2.
....

3.
....

4.
....

5.
....

Limited Liability Partnership (LLP)

This is a business structure that gives the benefits of limited liability but allows its members the flexibility of organising their internal structures such as in traditional partnerships. It has some similarities with ordinary partnership, as a number of individuals or limited companies share in the risks, costs, responsibilities, and profits of the business. Professional partnerships such as accountants and lawyers favour such a structure.

Are you considering the Limited Liability Partnership structure? If so, why?

....

....

....

....

....

....

....

What steps would you need to take to set up a limited liability partnership business model?

1. ....

2. ....

3. ....

4. ....

5. ....

Limited Liability Companies (LLC)

A limited liability company is a business with shareholders whose liability is limited by shares. This is among the most common form of privately held companies. One of the major distinguishing features is that personal finances or assets of the directors are distinct from company finances. However, directors may be required to guarantee loans or credit granted to the company. There are four main types of limited liability companies:

1. Private limited companies can have one or more shareholders. They cannot offer shares to the public. The liability of each member is limited to the amount unpaid on shares that a member holds.

2. Public limited companies (PLC), on the other hand, must have at least two shareholders and must have issued shares to the public to a value of at least £50,000 before it can trade. Liability of each member is limited to the amount unpaid on shares that a member holds. A PLC may offer its shares for sale to the general public and may also be quoted on the stock exchange.

3. Private unlimited companies are rare and usually created for specific reasons. It is recommended you take legal advice before creating one. This type of company may or may not have a share capital, and there is no limit to the members' liability. Because there is no limitation on members' liability, the company has to disclose less information than other types of companies.

4. Private companies limited by guarantee. With this type of company, members do not make any contribution to the capital during its lifetime as they do not purchase shares. The members' liability is limited to the amount that they each agree to contribute to the company's assets if it is wound up, closedown or cease doing business.

Are you considering the Limited Liability Company structure? If so, why?

What steps would you need to take to set up limited liability company business model?

1.

2.

3.

4.

5.

Franchise

Franchise is one of the business paths you can take if you are the type who is more comfortable with already tried and tested structures and systems, because with this type of structure, you buy a licence to use the name, products, services, and management support systems of the franchising company. It brings together the talents of the new business owner with the experience, knowledge, and track record of the franchiser. You are, therefore, granted the right to market an already established company's goods or services. You get to do business using the marketing methods, trademarked goods and services, and the goodwill and brand name already developed by the company within a certain geographical area. There is a common saying that with a franchise you are in business for yourself but not by yourself.

Many different types of business sectors use this structure. The most common franchised businesses are found in the food and drink industry. Examples include McDonalds, Subway, Starbucks, and Pizza Hut. However, other industries, such as hotel and travel, automotive, financial services, and cleaning and maintenance services, also operate under this business structure.

Are you considering the franchise structure? If so, why?

What steps would you need to take to set up a franchise business model?

1. ....

2. ....

3. ....

4. ....

5. ....

Social Enterprise

These are businesses with primarily social and environmental objectives. The authorities define them as "businesses with primarily social objectives whose surpluses are principally reinvested for that purpose in the business or in the community, rather than being driven by the need to maximise profit for shareholders and owners."

Are you considering the social enterprise structure? If so, why?

What steps would you need to take to set up a social enterprise business model?

1.

2.

3.

4.

5.

Deciding in favour of any of the above structures is very necessary for the future survival and growth of your business. Failing to adopt the best structure in the light of your needs and aspirations may lead to disappointments, especially when the tax man comes after you or you find yourself in a legal suit.

In the event of your business turning out profits without a properly adopted structure, the tax man is left to decide for you what is due him, and that can wipe away a lot of your hard-earned gains. On the other hand, in the event of a business failure, your liability can seriously affect your person. You could also lose out on benefits, such as writing off certain expenditures as business expenditures and other benefits you could have taken advantage of as a new or small business.

As you can see, it is in your interest to make a firm decision based on the features, advantages, and disadvantages I have provided for your consideration.

Chapter 7

Proven Winning Strategies For Growth

"Sound strategy starts with having the right goal..... Strategy is about making choices, trade-offs; it's about deliberately choosing to be different.... The company without a strategy is willing to try anything."

– Michael Porter
Professor at Harvard Business School, and a
leading authority on company strategy and the
competitiveness of nations and regions

A business strategy clearly helps you to articulate the direction a business will pursue and the steps it will take to achieve these goals. A good strategy should clearly differentiate a business from its competitors. Adopting or crafting a better strategy helps a business establish a clear framework for subsequent decisions, giving a business an edge in the marketplace right from the start. Your understanding of these strategies will help you choose the winning approach to success.

Marketing Strategy

A marketing strategy helps you identify and communicate the benefits of what your business offers to your target market, whereas a marketing plan helps you to simply implement your marketing strategy. A good marketing strategy should help you address the specific needs of the different customer groups. Contents of the marketing strategy should be measurable and actionable and work to differentiate your company and products from the competition. The objectives of your marketing strategy should also establish specific goals and must also take into account how your business strengths and weaknesses will affect your marketing.

So let's start to build a marketing strategy for your business by answering the following questions.

How do you define your business?

What are the products or services your business will provide or is providing?

Who are your target customers?

Which marketing category will you establish yourself in?

Does your business intend to become a market category leader, challenger, follower, or niche player?

What are the unique characteristics of your products or services that distinguish you from the competition?

What are your pricing policies? Will your price be above, below, or at parity with your competitors, and are you going to lead, follow, or ignore changes in competitors' pricing?

Through which distribution channels will your products or services be made available to the target market?

How will your advertising and promotions convey the unique characteristics of your product or service?

One of the most commonly used marketing strategies by new and small businesses is the growth strategy. The focus of this strategy is to simply help you identify the way you will use products and markets or customers to achieve a desired level of growth in your business. Which growth strategy fits your business?

Current product for current market. This strategy is used to increase your share of an already existing market. It is usually implemented by finding new customers or raising customers' awareness of your current products and services.

Is your current market fully aware of what you are offering?

Have you saturated your current market or geographical area?

Are there new customers you can access? Does your current market have capacity for more customers for your products or services?

Current product for new market. This is a strategy of finding and entering new markets with your current product or service. This new market could be a new segment of the market, a new country, or a new region.

Are there new markets available to your products and services?

$$\begin{array}{|l|}
\hline
\\[6pt]
\\[6pt]
\\[6pt]
\\[6pt]
\\[6pt]
\hline
\end{array}$$

Is this new market local, national or international?

Can your products or services be adapted to the needs of the new market?

New product for current market. This strategy approach simply demands you improve your existing products and services or develop new ones to enhance the benefits you deliver to your customers.

Do you have new products and services for your existing customers?

....
....
....
....

Is this a complimentary product or service to your existing business?

....
....
....
....

Is your current customer base your target market?

....
....
....
....

There is a bit more risk involved in adopting this strategy because you are more or less in uncharted territory, with totally new products for an entirely new market.

Marketing strategy can only benefit your business strategy if you use it. It is also important to ensure that you have the operational capacity and processes for fulfilling any extra orders, ensuring timely delivery, and providing any extra services efficiently and reliably in handling the extra business your strategy generates.

Pricing Strategy

Pricing strategies are sometimes not given much consideration by new businesses. However, they are a major determining factor in the survival or success of a business and a workable component of a good marketing strategy. Understanding this strategy and getting it right will positively affect your revenues and profit. For some businesses, it's simply looking at what is being charged by competitors and setting prices accordingly. A lower or higher price can significantly change both sales volumes and gross margins and, subsequently, profits.

Establishing your pricing objectives is undoubtedly among the most basic and important things to do. However, you can only accomplish the stated objectives after taking a variety of factors into consideration. "THE BUSINESS YOU CAN START – Spotting The Greatest Opportunities In The Economic Downturn" has more information for you to consider before answering the following questions.

Do you know your cost of production?

What steps do you need to take to determine your cost of production?

1.

2.

3.

4.

5.

Do you know what position you hold in the market?

What steps do you need to take to determine your position in the market?

1.

2.

3.

4.

5.

What steps do you need to take to determine the demand for your product or service?

1.

2.

3.

4.

5.

Environmental factors. It is equally important to find out what external factors may affect your pricing strategy. It is important to consider the implication of your pricing on your competitors. To set a price too low may be inviting an unpleasant risk of price wars. On the other hand, setting a price too high may attract a large number of competitors who want to share in the profits. Legally, a firm might not have total freedom in setting its price at any level. For instance, pricing too low may be considered predatory pricing, offering different prices for different consumers might be seen as price discrimination, or colluding with competitors to price a product or service may be illegal, which it is in most economies.

What steps do you need to take to determine what environmental factors could impact on your pricing strategy?

1.

2.

3.

4.

5.

The above factors should help you establish what your pricing objectives must be. The objectives could be:

◊ Seeking to maximize profit in the short run. This is not a very good objective if it results in lower long-term profits.

◊ Seeking to maximize current revenue with little regard for profit margins. This enables a business to increase its market share and lower cost now to ensure long-term profitability.

◊ Reducing long-term costs by maximizing the number of units sold or the number of customers served to increase profit in the long run.

◊ Maximizing profit margins on each unit of item sold. This is used particularly for items or products that are sold in small quantities, such as handmade automobiles and artwork.

◇ Using the price to signal high quality or a high level of service in an attempt to position the product as the quality leader. At the other extreme is to be the low-cost leader as a way of differentiating yourself from the competition.
◇ Surviving by covering just the cost. This is used especially when the market is in decline or over capacity.
◇ Seeking price stabilization just to avoid price wars and maintain a moderate and stable profit margin. Many new businesses do this.

What are your pricing objectives?

1.
....

2.
....

3.
....

4.
....

5.
....

With the understanding gained from the objectives and factors that should be considered in determining the price of a product, you should determine your pricing method. Again, there are options and it is important to establish that there is no one right way to price a product or service.

Finally, let me tie all the above together and give you a shot at some of the best strategies worth considering.

Cost plus mark-up. With this strategy, you decide the profit you want to make and add it to your cost to determine your selling price.

Competitive pricing. This is the opposite of cost plus mark-up. With this strategy, you use your competitors' prices as benchmarks to price your products or service. You could decide to price your products slightly above, below, or as your competitors, depending on your positioning strategy.

Trade discounting. This strategy seeks to attract business from profitable customer category (i.e. customer segment who contribute most of your profits) offering those special discounts, either as lower prices on certain products or free product rewards.

Loss leader. This involves selling below cost in order to attract more customers with the belief that they will buy other high-profit items. This is one strategy commonly used by most supermarkets.

Bundling and quantity discounts. This is where customers are rewarded for higher purchases through bundling or quantity discounts. It is done by setting the per-unit price lower should a customer purchase more instead of one, or charging less when a customer buys several related items in a single shopping trip.

Versioning. This is where you sell a general product in different configurations so the basic version is either offered free or at a very low price and the other services are available at a higher price.

Close out. This is best used when there is excess inventory to get rid of. The goal here should be to minimize losses instead of making profits. Stocks are sold at steep discounts to reduce or avoid storage cost.

Good pricing requires good market research. Find people

who will be potential customers of your products, understand their needs and provide what will meet their needs. Settle that, and determine your price based on your pricing objectives and existing or applicable factors to ensure the growth and profitability of your business. It is equally important to focus on adding value to your products as much as possible instead of relying solely on pricing in making your product much more competitive.

So my question for you is what is YOUR pricing strategy?

Advertising Strategy

"Nothing except the mint can make money without advertising."
-Thomas B. Macaulay

Every business needs to promote itself constantly in a way to reach out to its customers and potential customers. Advertising is basically the methods used by a business to publicize and position its products and services to its target market. This includes the use of salespeople, product launches, brand name and image, promotion of the product in retail and wholesale outlets, press releases and other public relations activities, and special offers.

Let's look at some of the methods or mediums by which you can advertise your business.

Many advertising methods are are discussed in "THE BUSINESS YOU CAN START – Spotting The Greatest Opportunities In The Economic Downturn"

including word of mouth, business cards, websites, TV, radio, trade shows and bus stops. You are most likely not going to be effective by using all of these methods. Your best shot will be to assess your advertising needs and choose the best option (some of which are almost free) with your objectives and budget in mind.

Which advertising media will work most effectively for YOUR business? Do you know why?

1.

2.

3.

4.

5.

Here are ten principles that can guide you in getting the best of effective advertising:

1. Use one message that is simple, catchy, short, easy to remember, and consistent. It must personally communicate to the individual reader. In the words of William Bernbach, a former advertising director, *"Advertising doesn't create a product advantage. It can only convey it."*

What is your advertising message?

2. Give your ad a relevant headline other than the name of your business. *"If your advertising goes unnoticed, everything else is academic."* William Bernbach

What is your advertising headline?

3. For effectiveness, focus and create unique ad messages for each specific audience or target group.

4. The message must communicate the benefits of what you are offering. Ensure your advertisement avoids bold claims that your product or service cannot deliver. *"Telling lies does not work in advertising."* Stanislaw Lec

What benefits do you want to convey in your advertising?

....

....

....

....

....

5. Create an ad that generates curiosity for customers to want to know more, even more than selling a product or service. In the words of Theodore Parker, *"Kodak sells film, but they don't advertise film. They advertise memories."*

How does your advertising message create curiosity?

....

....

....

....

....

6. All ads must have your contact details, such as telephone and fax numbers, e-mail addresses, websites, and company address, displayed very visibly.

Does your advertising message include all the relevant details?

....
....
....
....

7. Do not advertise via any medium just because your competitors are advertising in that medium.

8. Your ad must call its audience to take an action and show them where to start.

Does your advertising message have a call to action?

....
....
....
....
....

9. Negotiate with advertising houses based on what you pay for readership and audience, not just on what is quoted.

10. Constantly evaluate and test the effectiveness of your ads, and stop using a medium or method if it's not working. In the words of David Ogilvy, *"Never stop testing, and your advertising will never stop improving."*

How are you going to measure the effectiveness of your advertising message?

....
....
....
....
....
....
....

Sales Strategy

"Selling is a skill to master. You will ALWAYS be selling no matter what you do."

\- Karen Katz

As a new business, your commitment and enthusiasm to what you are going to sell is essential for your survival in the marketplace. Your ability to market your products and services will determine the success or failure of the business; however, for that to be possible, you must be able to sell effectively to generate revenues and profits.

A sales strategy is not the same as a marketing strategy. Your marketing strategy should enable you make yourself known to your market and get customers to be keen on what you are offering, and your sales strategy should help you "close the deal" with your customers. A sales strategy, properly implemented, should generate increased sales and enable you effectively establish yourself in the competition.

For a sales strategy to be relevant, it is important to have different sales strategies for each of your product lines, being conscious of the different customer groups or segments you will be selling to.

Here are a few steps that can guide you in putting together an effective sales strategy.

Set objectives. To start with, you must have objectives for your sales strategy. These objectives must be specific, measurable, achievable, realistic, and time-sensitive (SMART). Your focus can be on specific products or client groups.

What are your sales strategy goals?

```



```

Establish features and benefits. You must also distinguish clearly the unique features of your products and services and the benefits your customers will gain from buying them. Consider the product from your customers' perspective, and emphasize the different features from the benefits.

What are the features and benefits of your product or service ?

```




```

Understand competition. You need to also understand what your competitors are doing and how they are doing it. Evaluate their methods and establish what you can and should be doing differently.

What is your competition doing?

> ....
>
> ....
>
> ....
>
> ....

Define target market. A clearly defined target market is a must to enable you to sell strategically to generate revenues. Constantly evaluate your customer groups or segments, and design specific strategies to use in selling your products or services to each of them.

What is your target market? Do you have more than one?

> ....
>
> ....
>
> ....
>
> ....
>
> ....
>
> ....

Choose sales methods. You must now decide which sales methods to use to reach out to the various groups, after identifying them and establishing the benefits your products will bring to them. The nature of product you are selling and the geographical area should also help you determine which method will best enable you get to the customer to "close a deal." Some of the sales methods to use include direct face-to-face selling, telesales, Internet, and direct mail.

Present products well. It is very important to put resources and effort into how you are going to present your products or services to your customers. There is a popular saying that "you get what you see."

Have flexibility to negotiate. There must be a level of flexibility in your selling approach. You will need to be able to spot opportunities for the long term and be willing to cut down on your profit margin now by lowering your prices for repeat sales as well as promotional benefits.

Close the deal. This is where you persuade your customer, highlighting their need or want of what you are offering. It must not stop there. You must get a firm commitment, taking note of the ensuing negotiation, particularly listening to what the customer is saying.

Follow up. A good rapport with a customer should be a stepping-stone in following up on the sale. Follow-up confirms to the customer your faith in the product and the integrity of the benefits and features you sold to them. Requesting customer feedback can give you a clear insight into the exact mindset of your customer and can also give you further ideas for improvement on your product or service.

Using Social Media For Business

The use of social media has become very prominent in marketing products and services in the last couple of years, and I challenge you to explore it. It can be used to complement other methods of marketing and advertising without necessarily interfering with other mediums or methods. The benefits can be tremendous, but must be used in the most efficient way possible because not every business has the resources (time and money) or is ripe for marketing and advertising via this medium, at least not from the onset.

Using social media has basically become the online version of word-of-mouth marketing. Using it in the right way potentially will result in more customers, increased sales, and, thus, profit and growth and continuity of the business.

How can social media benefit YOUR business?

Facebook

Twitter

Instagram

Blogging

LinkedIn

....

....

....

....

....

Pinterest

....

....

....

....

Periscope

....

....

....

....

....

....

Chapter 8

Qualities of Successful Business People

"Whenever an individual or a business decides that success has been attained, progress stops."

– Thomas J. Watson
Former President of International Business Machines (IBM), who developed IBM's renowned management style and corporate culture

I have yet to come across a person in business who does not aspire to succeed in his or her chosen business. However, the desire to succeed is not a guarantee to becoming successful. There are certain characteristics and attitudes that distinguish those who have succeeded from those who are simply surviving. Not possessing any of these qualities does not in any way disqualify you from starting out. I believe most of these qualities can be developed over time should you set your mind to it. Choices, not circumstances, determine your success.

There are qualities required to be a successful business person and I have discussed them in "THE BUSINESS YOU CAN START – Spotting The Greatest Opportunities In The Economic Downturn". Read this section of the book and then spend some time on the following exercise in self-reflection.

Rate yourself on a scale of 0 - 10 on each of the skills needed to be successful in business (0 = no skill, 10 = a skill master). If you score below 5, write down one thing that you could do to improve this skill.

Desire:

Score ....

....
....

Passion:

Score ....

....
....

Purpose:

Score ....

Decision-making skills:

Score ....

Creative imagination:

Score ....

Leadership abilities:

Score ....

Self-starter:

Score ....

Higher goals:
Score . . . .

Self-determination:
Score . . . .

Judgement:
Score . . . .

Self confidence:
Score . . . .

Seeks solutions in the face of problems:
Score . . . .

Commitment:
Score . . . .

Patience:
Score . . . .

Realistic expectations:
Score . . . .

Risk taker:
Score . . . .

Perseverance:
Score . . . .

Personal and professional integrity:

Score . . . .

Driven by accomplishments, not money:

Score . . . .

Negotiation:

Score . . . .

Time management:

Score . . . .

Chapter 9

Business Skills and Knowledge to Develop

"Success always comes when preparation meets opportunity."

– Henry Hartman
A commercial graphic designer, illustrator
and fine art painter and drawer

In addition to personal qualities and skills, there are also certain business skills that can enhance your understanding of how to successfully start and manage a business. To some extent, Mitch Thrower, a business entrepreneur and author, was quite right in saying,

"Implementers don't care about the origins of ideas or the creative process; they are too busy with their own concerns, while idea people often don't value the necessary financial and business management skills necessary for execution."

However, for many new businesses, it is almost certain you will be both the originator of the idea and the implementer, at least in the initial stages. It is in your best interest to start by assessing your business knowledge and skills level. This will help you decide whether you need to learn new skills or draw on outside help by delegating, recruiting, or outsourcing aspects of the business not within your skill base to enable you focus on what you are more capable at. Having said that, developing these skills can help you better understand the business for effective and efficient management. Peter Drucker once made a distinction between efficient and effective business skills. He said,

"Performing an activity swiftly and economically is efficient, while doing the right thing well is effective."

The skills you need to focus on are discussed in "THE BUSINESS YOU CAN START – Spotting The Greatest Opportunities In The Economic Downturn". Read this section of the book and then spend some time on the following exercise in self-reflection.

Rate yourself on a scale of 0-10 on your business skills and knowledge. If you score below 5, write down one thing that you could do to improve this skill.

People management:

Score................

Product development:

Score................

Marketing skills:

Score................

Sales skills:

Score................

Supplier relationship management:

Score................

Financial management:

Score

Operations:

Score

Strategic management:

Score

Chapter 10

How to Put a Compelling Plan Together

"Before everything else, getting ready is the secret of success."

– Henry Ford
A prominent American industrialist and
founder of the Ford Motor Company

My experience in the field has exposed to me the level of confusion many associate with the subject of business planning. I find people who are honestly so intimidated with writing a business plan that they have never started the business they dreamt of. Others question its importance because they think it is only for securing external funding, and because they are not interested in any external funding they decide there is no need to consider putting one together. There are countless others who just never bothered about it. Some simply consulted their accountants or business advisors to write it for them. Unfortunately, for some of this last group of people, their presentations to bankers and investors were not convincing enough to secure the needed funding.

An international consultant, Dr. Graeme Edwards, once said,

"It's not the plan that is important, it's the planning."

A business plan is simply putting together a written document that describes a business, its objectives, its strategies, the market it is in, and its financial forecasts. It has both internal and external uses. For internal purposes, it can be used to help measure success, focus on development efforts, help spot potential pitfalls before they manifest, and structure the financial aspects of a business. On the other hand, it is used externally to introduce the business to or apply for funding from bankers, external investors (friends, venture capitalist firms), grant providers, potential buyers of the business, and potential partners.

Whichever way you look at it, the business plan is simply one of the most essential pieces of documentation that any person starting a business needs to consider putting together.

In the words of Chris Corrigan, an Australian businessman,

"You can't overestimate the need to plan and prepare. In most of the mistakes I've made, there has been this common theme of inadequate planning beforehand. You really can't over-prepare in business!"

For a new business, it is important to establish the purpose of the plan from the onset, because the emphasis of any plan should be dependent on the intended user.

In the next few pages, I am going to discuss the essential components of a typical business plan. This guide, when used with my uniquely designed template can help you write a compelling business plan. It will save you a lot of consultation hours. A typical plan includes the following but remember that it should be fine-tuned for your audience and purpose e.g. for raising capital, for bankers or investors.

As you read each section, use the template included in the appendices to complete your business plan.

I. Executive Summary

The executive summary is an overview of the business you want to start, a synopsis of the key points of your entire plan. It should include highlights from each section of the rest of the document, from the key features of the business opportunity to the elements of the financial forecasts.

The executive summary should be concise, no longer than two pages at most, and interesting. It is advisable to write the executive summary of your plan after you've completed the rest.

2. General Personal and Company Description

Personal details. Name, home address, telephone, mobile phone, date of birth, and marital status.

Business details. Business name, business address, telephone, e-mail, social media and website links.

Mission statement. Many companies have a brief mission statement, usually in thirty words or fewer, explaining their reasons for being and their guiding principles. If you want to draft a mission statement, this is a good place to put it in the plan.

Company goals and objectives. Goals are destinations. Objectives are progress markers along the way to goal achievement.

Business philosophy. What is important to you in business?

To whom will you market your products? State it briefly, it should be dealt with more thoroughly in the Marketing Plan section.

Describe your industry. Is it a growth industry? What changes do you foresee in the industry, short-term and long-term? How will your company be poised to take advantage of them?

Describe your most important company strengths and core competencies. What factors will make the company succeed? What do you think your major competitive strengths will be? What background experience, skills, and strengths do you personally bring to this new venture?

Legal form of ownership. Sole proprietor, partnership, corporation, limited liability company or corporation? Why have you selected this form?

Exit strategy. You may want to explain to investors how they will get their money back, what you are anticipating they will recover in excess of their investment, and in what time frame.

Possible exit strategies can include the sale or merger of your company, a management buyout, an IPO, or a private placement.

3. Products and Services

Describe in depth your products or services. Technical specifications, drawings, photos, sales brochures, and other bulky items belong in Appendices. Discuss pricing, service, support, warranty and production and include the advantages of your products or services, and how they compare to the competition.

4. Marketing Plan

RESEARCH

Why? It is quite deceptive to assume that you already know about your intended market. You need to do market research to make sure you are on track. Use the opportunity to uncover data and to question your marketing efforts.

How? There are two kinds of market research: primary and secondary.

Primary research means gathering your own data.

Secondary research means using published information, such as industry profiles, trade journals, newspapers, magazines, census data, and demographic profiles. This type of information is available in public libraries, industry associations, chambers of commerce, from vendors who sell to your industry, and from government agencies.

In your marketing plan, be as specific as possible: about your industry give statistics, numbers, and sources. The marketing plan will be the basis later on of all important sales projections.

What barriers to entry do you face in entering this market with your new company? Some typical barriers may include:

How will you overcome the barriers? How could the following affect your company?

5. Products

In the *Products and Services* section, you described your products and services as you see them. Now, describe them from your customers' points of view.

Features and benefits. List all of your major products or services.

What after-sale services will you give? Some examples are delivery, warranty, service contracts, support, follow-up, and refunds.

6. Customers

Identify your targeted customers, their characteristics, and their geographic locations, i.e., their demographics. Then, for each customer group, construct what is called a demographic profile, including age, gender, location, income level, social class, occupation, and education level. For business customers, the demographic factors might be industry, location, size of firm, quality, technology, and price preferences.

7. Competition

List your major competitors (names and addresses). Will they compete with you across the board, or just for certain products, certain customers, or in certain locations?

Will you have important indirect competitors? How will your products or services compare with the competition?

Other areas to consider: niche, marketing strategy, promotion, promotional budget, pricing (explain your methods of setting prices), proposed location, and distribution channels (how you sell your products or services: retail, direct (mail order, web, catalog), wholesale, your own sales force, agents, independent representatives, bid on contracts).

8. Sales Forecast

It's time to attach some numbers to your plan. Use a sales forecast spreadsheet to prepare a month-by-month projection. Forecast should be based on your historical sales, the marketing strategies that you have just described in your market research, and industry data, if available.

You may want to do two forecasts:

- ◇ A "best guess," which is what you really expect.
- ◇ A "worst case" low estimate that you are confident you can reach no matter what happens.

Remember to keep notes on your research and your assumptions as you build this sales forecast and all subsequent spreadsheets in the plan. This is critical if you are going to present it to funding sources.

9. SWOT Analysis

A SWOT analysis simply helps you to assess your *Strengths* and *Weaknesses*, and the *Opportunities* and *Threats* your business faces or may face in the course of operations. It provides a clear basis for examining your business performance.

10. Operational Plan

Explain the daily operation of the business, its location, equipment, people, processes, and surrounding environment.

Production. How and where are your products or services produced?

Location. What qualities do you need in a location? Describe the type of location you'll have.

Legal environment. Licensing and bonding requirements, permits, health, workplace, or environmental regulations, special regulations covering your industry or profession, etc.

Personnel. Number of employees, type of labour, where you find the right employees. Quality of existing staff, pay structure, training methods and requirements, task breakdown, etc.

Inventory. What kind of inventory will you keep: raw materials, supplies, finished goods? Average value in stock (i.e. what is your inventory investment). Rate of turnover and how this compares to the industry averages. Seasonal buildups. Lead time for ordering.

Suppliers. Identify key suppliers, with names and addresses, type and amount of inventory furnished, credit and delivery policies, history, and reliability.

Credit policies. Do you plan to sell on credit? Do you really need to sell on credit? Is it customary in your industry and expected by your clientele? If yes, what policies will you have about who gets credit and how much? How will you check the creditworthiness of new applicants? What terms will you offer your customer— that is, how much credit, and when will payment be due?

Managing your accounts receivable. If you do extend credit, you should do an ageing report (a list of customers' accounts receivable amounts by how long they are owed) to alert management to any slow paying customers at least monthly.

Managing your accounts payable. You should also age your accounts payable, what you owe to your suppliers. This helps you plan whom to pay and when. Paying too early depletes your cash, but paying late can cost you valuable discounts and can damage your credit.

11. Management and Organization Plan

◇   This section of the plan should include:
◇   Biographic summary of key management
◇   Organizational charts (current and future)
◇   Manpower table
◇   Board of advisors
◇   Board of directors

If you'll have more than ten employees, create an organizational chart showing the management hierarchy and who is responsible for key functions. Include position descriptions for key employees. If you are seeking loans or investors, include resumes (in the Appendices) of owners and key employees.

12. Personal Financial Statement

Include personal financial statements for each owner and major stockholder, showing assets and liabilities held outside the business and personal net worth. Owners will often have to draw on personal assets to finance the business, and these statements will show what is available. Bankers and investors usually want this information as well.

It is also important that thought goes into the amount of money that you require per month to maintain your current standard of living, let alone improve it. The business needs to know how much you require so that pricing decisions can be realistically made.

13. Start-Up Expenses and Capitalization

You will have quite a number of expenses before you even begin operating your business. It is important to estimate these expenses accurately and then to plan where you will get sufficient capital.

Explain your research and how you arrived at your forecasts of expenses. Give sources, amounts, and terms of proposed loans. Also explain in detail how much will be contributed by each investor and what percent ownership each will have.

14. Financial Plan

The financial plan may consist of twelve months' or one to five years' profit and loss projection, a cash-flow projection, a projected balance sheet, and a break-even calculation. Together, they constitute a reasonable estimate of your company's financial future. More importantly, the process of thinking through the financial plan will improve your insight into the inner financial workings of your company.

Projected cashflow. If the profit projection is the heart of your business plan, cash flow is the blood. Businesses fail because they cannot pay their bills. Every part of your business plan is important, but none of it means a thing if you run out of cash. *Sample forecast Cash Flow Statement can be found as Appendix II.*

Profit and loss statement. The primary tool for good financial reporting is the profit and loss statement. This is a measure of a company's sales and expenses over a specific period of time. It is prepared at regular intervals (monthly for the first year and annually through five years) to show the results of operating during those accounting periods. It should follow generally accepted accounting principles and must contain specific revenue and expense categories regardless of the nature of the business. *Sample forecast Profit and Loss Statement can be found as Appendix III.*

Opening day balance sheet. A balance sheet is one of the fundamental financial reports that any business needs for reporting and financial management. A balance sheet shows what items of value are held by the company (assets) and what its debts are (liabilities). When liabilities are subtracted from assets, the remainder is owners' equity. *Sample forecast Balance Sheet Statement can be found as Appendix IV.*

Break-even analysis. A break-even analysis predicts the sales volume, at a given price, required to recover total costs. The sales level is the dividing line between operating at a loss and operating at a profit. Expressed as a formula, break-even is:

Breakeven Sales = Fixed Costs - Variable Costs

where fixed costs are expressed in dollars, but variable costs are expressed as a percent of total sales.

15. Appendices

Include details and studies in your business plan. For example, include:

⋄ Brochures and advertising materials
⋄ Industry reports and information
⋄ Forecasted profit and loss statement
⋄ Forecasted cash-flow statement
⋄ Blueprints and plans, maps and photos of location
⋄ Magazine articles or other articles
⋄ Detailed lists of equipment owned or to be purchased
⋄ Copies of leases and contracts
⋄ Letters of support from future customers
⋄ Any other materials needed to support the assumptions
⋄ in this plan,
⋄ Market research studies
⋄ List of assets available as collateral for a loan

Chapter 11

Conclusion

The ability to seize opportunities by connecting problems and questions with solutions and answers and turning them into viable money-making business ventures is one of the most creative things any individual can do to transform his or her life. Mary Lou Cook, an American educationist, once said,

"Creativity is inventing, experimenting, growing, taking risks, breaking rules, making mistakes, and having fun."

Interestingly, opportunities do not often show up with labels and signposts. The big ones we tend to wish for and daydream about seldom come by and, if any turn up, the chances of accessing them and owning them are very slim. Jumping at several smaller opportunities daily has proven over time to be the better prospect. If you ignore a chance, someone else will surely find it.

Unfortunately, they will be the ones to enjoy the fruits should the idea succeed. Being creative as you go about your daily activities and engaging your brain can help you solve almost every problem there is in life. And you will be glad to know that life only pays you for the problems you solve. Woody Allen, an American screenwriter, director, and author, sums it up this way,

"Summing up, it is clear the future holds great opportunities. It also holds pitfalls. The trick will be to avoid the pitfalls, seize the opportunities, and get back home by six o'clock."

Step-by-Step Checklist

Here's a quick rundown of the basic steps to a great start in starting and growing a business.

1. *Have a clear idea of:*

    a. Product or service. What your USP (Unique Selling Point) will be. Be passionate about it. (refer to Chapters 2 and 4)

    b. Branding. Choose a name, logo, and slogan consistent with your aim and target audience. Ensure quality designs of letterhead, business cards, etc.

    c. Your target group.

    d. Market research.

2. **Develop the idea with the customer in mind, as well as yourself and your ability to compete.** (refer to Chapter 3)

3. *Decide the business model. Office, home-based, licensing, multi-level marketing, drop shipping?* (refer to Chapter 5)

4. *Decide on where to start from: part time or full time?*

5. *Decide how you will produce the product or supply the service.*

6. **Check out any regulations and licenses involved.** (refer to Chapter 6)

7. *Decide how much to charge for your product or service.* (refer to Chapter 7)
8. *Decide how to market and sell your product or service:* direct mail, telemarketing, designing and printing (flyers, brochures, etc.), exhibitions, websites, research, surveys, promotions, press releases, public relations, photography, and advertising. (Chapter 7)

9. *Decide the legal structure (sole trader, partnership, limited liability company, etc.) that will favour you.* Register the business where necessary. Resolve who will manage the business. (Chapter 6)

10. *Decide on your capital requirement and how to fund it.* It will be in your interest to prepare a cash-flow and profit and loss forecast for twelve months or one to five years, or both.

11. *Get to know basic information about taxes,* National Insurance, salaries and wages, and business rates.

12. *Do everything possible to put your business plan together, either as a formal document or in any informal way you choose to write it* (refer to Chapter 10).

Finally, thank you for getting a copy of this workbook. I hope you have taken, or are about to take, the necessary steps to start out. According to Geri Weitzman, an American author and psychologist,

> *"Sometimes you gotta create what you want to be a part of."*

Go for it, and you will succeed one way or the other.

Appendix

Appendix I
Business Plan

EXECUTIVE SUMMARY

Is an overview of the business you want to start. It is a synopsis of the key points of your entire plan. It should include highlights from each section of the rest of the document - from the key features of the business opportunity through to the elements of the financial forecasts.

Its purpose is to explain the basics of your business in a way that both informs and interests the reader. If, after reading the executive summary, an investor or manager understands what the business is about and is keen to know more, it has done its job.

It should be concise - no longer than two pages at most - and interesting. It's advisable to write this section of your plan after you've completed the rest.

PERSONAL DETAILS

Name: ....

Home Address: ....
....
....
....
....

Telephone: .... Mobile: ....

Date of Birth: ....

Marital Status: ....

BUSINESS DETAILS

Business Name: ....

Business Address: ....
....
....
....
....

Telephone: .... Fax: ....

Mobile: .... E-mail: ....

BUSINESS DESCRIPTION

This section should include a concise description of: What you intend to do, How you intend to do it and why you feel there is a market. It should be brief.

PERSONAL AIMS AND OBJECTIVES

Use this space to outline your personal aims and objectives concerning the business i.e. to establish and maintain a strong business that increases production by 10% per annum.

EDUCATION AND QUALIFICATIONS

Please include all qualifications including vocational, overseas etc.

TRAINING RECORD/ CERTIFICATES/ AWARDS

PREVIOUS EMPLOYMENT/ EXPERIENCE

OTHER EXPERIENCE/ INTERESTS

REFERENCES

_____
_____
_____
_____
_____
_____
_____
_____
_____
_____
_____
_____

MARKET RESEARCH

To put it simply, without a market there is no business. With this in mind, it is essential that time and effort is put into locating and assessing the market for your product or service. It is important to evaluate the size of the potential market (who are your customers), existing competition (and their strengths and weaknesses), and what advantages your product or service will have over the competition.

Remember that this information is not just to be found out and ignored. To build a strong business it is important to use the information that you collect in an effective manner: for example, a competitor's product has a certain design, can it be improved upon and if so can you do it?

CUSTOMERS

Who are your customers going to be? What age range are you aiming at? Where will you find them?

COMPETITORS

Who are your competitors? What do they sell? What do they charge? What are their strengths and weaknesses?

ADVANTAGES

What advantages do you have over your competitors? Is your product superior in some way? Is location an advantage? Etc.

PRODUCTS/ SERVICES

Your whole business revolves around your products/services. Use this section to outline the range of products/services you intend to offer and how you could develop them in the future.

PRICING STRATEGY

Your pricing strategy is a vital part of your overall business plan. You must know what your competitors are charging and be competitive with this price. This does not necessarily mean undercutting, but by having unique selling points – perhaps your quality is better but priced closely to a competitors. Will you charge by the hour or by the job?

PLACE/PREMISES

Where will your business be located? What are the costs of renting a shop or workshop? How long will you need to lease for? What if you need to expand, what equipment will you need? Use this space to answer these questions.

PROMOTION

Use this space to highlight how you intend to promote/advertise your product/service. How much will promotion cost?

....
....
....
....
....
....
....
....
....

PEOPLE

It is important to be aware of the people that you need to help you to succeed; this may include people working directly for you or people working for you indirectly such as an accountant or solicitor. Do not forget yourself, as you are the more important person in your business. What skills do you have, how can they be enhanced, and what training might you need?

....
....
....
....
....
....
....

S Strengths

W Weaknesses

O Opportunities

T Threats

CAPITAL REQUIREMENTS

How much money are you going to need to set up your business? Remember this will include the money for premises (buying or leasing) making those premises suitable for your business (even if working from home you may need to convert a room into an office), any equipment you may need, and working money to get you through those first lean months as the business becomes established.

Premises		
Details of Premises	Tenure	
Refurbishment		
Nature of Work		
Equipment and Vehicles		
Details (indicate new or used)		
Working Capital		
TOTAL CAPITAL REQUIREMENTS		

SOURCES OF CAPITAL

Where will you get the money that you need to start up your business? Do you have money of your own? Can your family help you? Can you get a loan from the bank? Can you get a grant? Can you crowdfund? Look at all the options, rates of interest, control and decision making implications, etc. Check out my book "Pitch Your Business Like a Pro" for in-depth analysis on your funding options and how to win investor support for business.

DETAILS		AMOUNT
Own Resources		
Grant		
Loan		
Loan Facility		
Overdraft Facility		
Other		
CAPITAL AVAILABLE		

SURVIVAL INCOME

It is important that thought goes into the amount of money that you require per month to maintain your current standard of living, let alone improve it. The business needs to know how much you require so that pricing decisions etc. can be realistically made. Use the form below to work out how much you and your family need per month.

ESTIMATED EXPENDITURE	AMOUNT £
Mortgage/Rent	
Council Tax	
Water Rates	
Heat/Light	
Personal, Property Insurance	
Housekeeping – Food etc.	
Clothing	
Telephone	
Entertainment	
Car Tax/ Insurance	
Car Running Expenses	
Family Expenditure/Presents	
Hire Charges	
HP Repayment	
Savings Plans	
Newspapers/Magazines	
Special Occasions	
Holidays	
Other	
Total Monthly Outgoing	
Other Family Income e.g. benefits, wages, etc.	
Monthly Survival Income	

NOTES

DATE: _____

SIGNED: _____

(Company Name / Logo)

Appendix 11
Sample Forecast Cash Flow Statement

	Pre-Startup	Month 1	Month 2	Month 3	Month 4	Month 5	Month 6	Month 7	Month 8	Month 9	Month 10	Month 11	Month 12	Total
	£	£	£	£	£	£	£	£	£	£	£	£	£	£
Receipts														
Owners' Capital														
Bank Loan / Cash Injection														
Sales														
Government Grant														
Total Cash Rcpts														
OVERHEADS														
Purchases														
Salaries														
Emp National Insurance														
Office Expenses														
Rent														
Telephone														
Business Rate														
Water Rates														
Subscription														
Bank Charges & Interest														
General Expenses														
Training & Development														
Heating & Lighting														
Insurance														
Loan Repayment														
Advertising														
Marketing														
Professional Fees														
Delivery Charges														
Travel Expenses														
Vehicle Running Cost														
General Maintenance														
Registration Fees														
Professional Fees														
Capital Equipment														
Fixtures & Fittings														
Stock														
Market Research														
Marketing														
Refurbishment														
Total Overheads														
Monthly Cash flow														
Opening Bal														
Closing Bal														

Appendix III
Sample forecast Profit and Loss Statement

	£		%
Sales			
Cost/Goods Sold (COGS)			
Gross Profit			
Less Overheads			
Salaries			
Emp National Insurance			
Office Expenses			
Rent			
Telephone			
Business Rate			
Water Rate			
Subscription			
Bank Charges and Interest			
General Expenses			
Training & Development			
Heat and Light			
Insurance			
Loan Repayment			
Marketing			
Advertising			
Accounting and Legal Fees			
Delivery Charges			
Travel Expenses			
Vehicle Running Cost			
General Repairs & Maintenance			
Taxes			
Depreciation Furniture			
Depreciation on Equipment			
Depreciation on Vehicle			
Other Expense (specify)			
Net Profit before Tax			

Appendix VI
Sample forecast Profit and Loss Statement

As at December 20___

Assets	
Current assets	
Cash	
Petty cash	
Accounts receivable	
Stock	
Short-term investment	
Prepaid expenses	
Long-term investment	
Fixed assets	
Land	
Buildings	
Improvements	
Equipment	
Furniture	
Motor vehicles	
Total assets	
Liabilities	
Current liabilities	
Accounts payable	
Interest payable	
Taxes payable	
Income tax	
Sales tax	
Payroll accrual	
Long-term liabilities	
Borrowings	
Total liabilities	
Net assets	
Owner's equity	
Retained earnings	
Current year earnings	
Total equity (should equal net assets)	

Other Titles From The Author

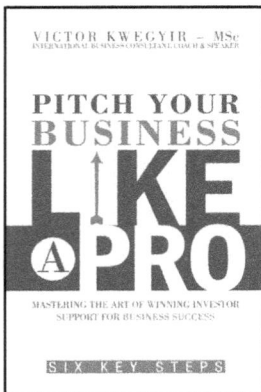

All books are available in EBook and Paperback formats on all major bookseller platforms worldwide - Amazon, Barnes and Nobles, Gardners, Ingram, iBookstore, Kindle, Kobo, WHSmith and many more. You can also order your copies by visiting www.victorkwegyir.com / www.vikesprings.com. Thank you for your continued support. Your success is our motivation.